To Eric love from J + M.

LOWESTOFT
Now & Then

Jack Rose
and
Dean Parkin

Rushmere
Publishing

Acknowledgements

We would like to thank all those who helped during the course of this book, especially Ron Ashby, Simon and Diane Baker, Alison Meadows, Pamela Graystone, Terry Lines, Roger Breeds, Ivan Meadows, Robin and Liz Summers, John Holmes, Ada Jones, Dennis Meadows and Heather Parkin for giving their time and effort in pursuit of information or photographs for us.

Thanks are due once again to Bert Collyer for his continuing help and we are also very grateful to the following for permission to reprint their photographs; Peter Calvert, Simon Baker, Ron Ashby, Molly O'Shea, Mick Howes, Nancy Solomon, Joan Reynolds, Ruth Ford, David Porter, Bob Blizzard, Geoff Dann, Margaret Price, Richard Ecclestone, John Ward, Mark Burrell, Michael Foreman, Ray Wharton, ECN Picture Library, May Elliston, Mike Veale, Dennis Lines, Vina Capps-Jenner, Mandy Prentice, Kenny Carsey, Tony Wilson, David Chipperfield, John Catchpole, Mark Pearce, Megan Goodall, Ann Jeffries and Michael Leslie

A special word of thanks must go to Mick Howes, for his pictures which appear on pages 9, 107 (bottom) and 113 (top) and also to Peter Calvert for his contribution to this book. Peter has supplied us with many of the modern and more recent photographs, and we are extremely grateful and pleased to be able to use his work in this publication.

This book is dedicated to Molly O'Shea.

Copyright © 1999 Rushmere Publishing

First published 1999 by Rushmere Publishing
32 Rushmere Road, Carlton Colville, Lowestoft, Suffolk NR33 8DA

Printed and typeset in England by Blackwell John Buckle
Charles Street, Great Yarmouth, Norfolk NR30 3LA

ISBN 1 872992 14 5 (paperback)
ISBN 1 872992 19 6 (hardback)

Contents

20th Century Review

Panoramic view of modern Lowestoft, showing Waveney Dock and the Fish Market in the foreground whilst just beyond that is Battery Green Road and the Hippodrome which was destroyed by fire in 1999.

Early twentieth century view of Lowestoft's swing bridge with the harbour cottages on the right, where the Harbour Master lived. The swing bridge was opened in 1897 and the townspeople turned out in force to celebrate the structure's arrival as they had been grumbling about the previous bridge for years - it was narrow, single track and operated by four men turning two cranks!

London Road North in the Edwardian era. The building on the right is the London and Provincial Bank which opened here in 1898 and amalgamated with Barclays Bank in 1918, moving further up London Road North in 1923. This corner site was bought by Tuttle's which first moved into this row in 1888 and gradually acquired the neighbouring premises.

Lowestoft's first tram car makes its way down London Road South, driven by the Mayor at the opening ceremony on Wednesday July 22nd, 1903. It was originally intended that the line should run along Marine Parade but 'in deference to the wish of the residents, expressed in an extensively signed petition' the route was changed to London Road South. However, in July 1902 the Lowestoft Journal reported a change of mind, '... it is now stated that many of those who signed the petition have changed their minds and would like the trams to run by the route which was at first suggested. Well, if that is the case, one can only pity them. They should have made sure that they knew what they wanted ...!'

1900-10

1900 Empire Hotel built - Morton's established. **1901** Population according to census 23,385 - Marina Theatre opened - Electrical Works opened in Norwich Road. **1902** South Cliff Congregational Church built - Lowestoft's first sea wall built - Stella Maris Church opened - Beach Bethel opened - Victoria Arcade in London Road North built. **1903** Claremont Pier built - Tram route established - Hamilton Dock opened. **1904** Hippodrome opened. **1905** Carnegie Library built in Clapham Road. **1907** Belle Vue Park and Sparrow's Nest enlarged - Chadd's established - Street lighting introduced in the town. **1910** Secondary School, Yarmouth Road (later Denes High School) opened.

1911-19

1911 Population 37,886. **1913** Record number of 535 million herrings landed at Lowestoft - Town's first cinema, The Palace, opened - Sparrow's Nest Theatre opened. **1914** World War I broke out - Central School built on Whapload Road. **1915** German Zeppelins a constant threat to the town, dropping bombs on three occasions. **1916** Lowestoft bombarded by German Naval Squadron. **1917** Tom Crisp posthumously awarded the Victoria Cross after his armed smack was attacked by a German U-boat. **1918** World War I ended. **1919** Oulton Broad was incorporated with Lowestoft - Welcome home feast held on the Denes for 3,500 soldiers to celebrate the end of World War I.

Lowestoft yacht basin in 1999 (above) and in the first decade of the twentieth century (below). A guide book from 1914 states that at the time the yacht basin was regarded as one of the best and most convenient in England. 'Yachts of any tonnage can enter at all states of the tide and on a summer evening dozens of craft may be seen at their moorings - from the magnificently appointed steam yachts to the flying cutter - their owners and crews listening to the strains of the military bands which play upon the nearby Pier daily in the evening.'

1920-29

1920 Empire Hotel renamed St. Luke's. **1921** Town's population was 44,323 - Religious revival in the town - War memorial erected on Royal Plain. **1922** Kensington Gardens opened. **1923** New sea wall built - Lowestoft school teachers' strike. **1924** Normanston Park bought by the Town Council. **1925** Denes Oval laid out. **1926** Jack Rose born. **1927** First motor buses in the town. **1928** Howard Hollingsworth gave Nicholas Everitt Park to the town. **1929** Everitt's Park opened to public - CWS food factory opened.

1930-39

1931 Population 41,769 - The last tram ran in Lowestoft - Earth tremor felt - Outdoor swimming pool built on the Denes - St. John's Church was the venue for the first concert by a young Benjamin Britten. **1933** May 8th: The Town Hall Riot. The unemployed and police clashed in the Town Hall during a march protesting about a cut in allowances - The Beach Village was declared a slum clearance area and a council estate planned in its place. **1934** Notley Road School, now Kirkley High School, was opened - Pakefield incorporated with Lowestoft. **1935** Town's children paraded on the Oval to commemorate the Silver Jubilee of King George V. **1937** Odeon Cinema opened - Town tank, which stood next to the lighthouse, was sold for scrap - Windmill at Oulton Broad demolished. **1938** Lowestoft Lighthouse switches from oil to electricity. **1939** Outbreak of World War II - First siren sounded 11.00am 3rd September - Mayor Barraclough died, Major Selwyn Woolaston Humphrey takes the job - Evacuation of schoolchildren from London to Lowestoft - New Mutford Bridge opened.

Kirkley Cliff Road in the 1920s.

London Road, Pakefield, in the 1930s, with the *Tramways* public house in the distance on the left. With the tram lines taken up, the town moved into the era of buses.

Jubilee Parade was built in 1935 at a cost of £60,000.

1940-49

1940 Harry Dowsett bought Brooke's - June: evacuation of school children from Lowestoft to the Midlands - The town's peacetime population of 44,000 was halved during wartime - July: Co-op shop in Clapham Road destroyed in an air-raid which resulted in four people being killed - The bombing continues. **1941** 13th January: Worst raid of the war, four bombs fall on London Road North, seventy people killed - All Saints Church, Pakefield, destroyed by a bomb - Direct hits on the power house of the swing bridge, the Custom House, Harbour Master's residence and harbour works result in ten being killed - Carnegie Library in Clapham Road destroyed in a raid. **1942** Normanhurst taken over as fire station - Six bombs fell on Till Road, Summer Road and Stanley Street. Fifteen killed - Mayor Humphrey awarded the O.B.E. **1943** May: Thirty-three dead in a raid on north Lowestoft. **1944** London children evacuated to Lowestoft again due to the new menace of flying bombs. **1945** 30th April: Last air raid sounded at 1.25pm - Major Humphrey, Mayor throughout the war, resigned. **1946** The sea wall collapsed and subsequently a new one was built. **1947** Mrs. MacBain Taylor became first lady Mayor of Lowestoft. **1948** Lowestoft Railway taken over by British Rail. **1949** Birds Eye open a small depot in the town.

1950-59

1950 Public library moved to Suffolk Road. **1951** Population 42,834 - T.V. Manufacturing was established in the town. **1952** Birds Eye opened a complete production unit in the town. **1953** East coast floods caused loss of life and property damage - Royal Naval Patrol Service Memorial unveiled in Belle Vue Park. **1955** Victorian Pavilion on the South Pier demolished and replaced - First stage of the slum clearance

A young Michael Caine joined the repertory company at the Arcadia Theatre in 1955. 'It was a lovely theatre,' Michael recalled in his autobiography and during his stay in the town he married the leading lady, Patricia Haines, at the town's registry office. The theatre is now The Hollywood Cinema.

View from the South Pier in January 1973, with the Royal Hotel on the left and St. John's Church on the right.

programme announced with the Beach Village to be demolished. **1956** Central Methodist Church in London Road North demolished as a result of damage during the war. **1958** St. Luke's demolished. **1959** Slum clearance continued, resulting in the demolition of streets in north Lowestoft.

1960-69

1960 Tuttle's was taken over by Debenham's. **1961** Population 45,730 - The Town Council debated the 'Yartoft' proposals for a merger with Great Yarmouth. **1962** Gasworks closed. **1963** Normanston House demolished - Blundeston Prison opened. **1964** Lowestoft drifters the first in the country to be equipped with television. **1965** Lowestoft College of Further Education opened. **1966** Palace Cinema destroyed by fire. **1967** East Suffolk Police, one of the oldest constabularies in the country, merged with Ipswich & West Suffolk Police - Town's three remaining gas lamps extinguished for the last time - St. Peter's Court, Lowestoft's only high rise tower block, built - Herring fishery ended. **1968** The town's first office computer lifted by crane into the offices of Small & Co. **1969** The old swing bridge jammed in the open position - Closure of Lowestoft to Great Yarmouth railway line announced.

1970-79

1970 Ada Roe dies shortly before her 112th birthday - Trinity Methodist Church opened. **1971** Population 50,610 - New fire station in Normanston Drive opened - New industrial buildings erected on the cleared site of the Beach Village - Two cannons, which had been buried at the Corporation depot during World War II for safekeeping, were discovered and restored and replaced in Belle Vue Park. **1972** Suffolk Hotel demolished - Current harbour bridge opened.

(Above) A 1990s view of Mutford Lock and the Wherry Hotel. The small timber bridge for pedestrians and cycles was also built as part of the redevelopment scheme. Mutford Lock is unique because it is the only one in existence possessing eight pairs of gates, necessary because of the difference in the height of water in the salt and freshwater sides of the lock.

(Left) In November 1992 the new Mutford Bridge and restored lock gates were officially opened. A flotilla of boats, including the wherry *Hathaw*, were there for the occasion making their way through the lock to Lake Lothing accompanied by a lone trumpeter who played 'Sailing' and 'Rule Britannia'. This was the eighth bridge here, replacing a structure which had been in service since 1939.

The Hippodrome bingo hall was destroyed by fire late on Sunday 31st January 1999. One hundred and fifty firemen from twenty-five brigades fought to control the flames with water pumped from the Trawl Dock but, although adjacent properties were saved, by the following morning only the walls of the Hippodrome were left, with the interior and roof reduced to smoking remains.

The Hippodrome was built in 1904 and since then has been put to many uses such as a permanent circus, a cinema, a variety playhouse and even a centre for wartime evacuees. Soon after the fire plans were made for the rebuilding of the bingo hall early in the new century. The adjoining premises, formerly the Gourock Ropeworks but now Ananas and Dansk's pine furniture shop, also suffered fire and water damage in the spectacular blaze, which was said to have been one of the worst in Lowestoft for many years.

1973 Royal Hotel demolished - Last train ran from fish market to station - Baptist Church demolished in London Road North (moved to a new church in London Road South). **1974** Donald Durrant became the town's last Mayor - Borough of Lowestoft became Waveney District Council. **1975** New library opened in Clapham Road - St. Peter's Church demolished. **1977** Brooke Marine was nationalised. **1978** 6th May: The wrecking of oil tanker the *Eleni V* caused massive oil slicks on beaches from Winterton to Lowestoft - Benjamin Britten High School opened - St. John's Church demolished - New roads and a one-way system opened in central Lowestoft. **1979** Odeon Cinema demolished - New Police Station opened in Old Nelson Street

1980-89

1980 Catling's demolished to make way for a new supermarket - Hailey's store in London Road South damaged by fire, never re-opened. **1981** Population 54,907 - Tuttle's store closed after 138 years trading in the town. **1983** Pleasurewood Hills opened. **1984** Completion of the pedestrianisation of London Road North. **1985** Queen visited Lowestoft to officially open shopping precinct - Brooke Marine privatised. **1986** The trawler *Pescado* capsized with the loss of three men, leaving one survivor. **1987** Richard Branson's Virgin Atlantic Challenger II built at Brooke's yard - New Fish Market opened. **1988** Brooke Marine wound up but Brooke Yachts buy the shipyard - Britten Centre opened - New lifeboat bought with money raised by the town - Morton's factory closed - The 'Armada Post' in Martin's Score replaced and renewed. **1989** The South Pier Pavilion demolished - Hollywood Cinema opened in the former Arcadia Theatre.

Jack Rose (centre) with his late friends, Trevor Westgate (left) and Wally Holden (right) at the Charter Day Ceremony in 1985 when Jack received the 'Distinguished Citizen' award.

The Britten Centre shopping area under construction in 1987.

1990-1999

1990 North Quay Shopping Park opened, built on the former site of Eastern Coachworks. **1991** Population 57,122 - Sparrow's Nest Theatre demolished. **1992** The new Mutford Bridge opened. **1993** Birds Eye open Denes IV factory - East Point Pavilion built - Artillery Way built. **1994** Richards' shipyard closed - CWS canning factory closed. **1995** The Lowestoft War Memorial Museum opened in Sparrow's Nest Park. **1996** Jarrold's closed after nearly ninety years in the town. **1997** Triangle Market, High Street, relocated as part of a wider scheme. **1998** CCTV security cameras put up around the town. **1999** Hippodrome destroyed by fire - New boathouse for lifeboat built - Wellington Gardens laid out - Scores refurbished.

Hailey's Court was built on the site of the old department store after which it is named. The clock which can be seen over the building's entrance was erected in 1999. Called the 'Millennium Clock', it was paid for by the South Lowestoft Traders Association and some of the area's oldest residents attended its unveiling.

Crowds gather for the opening of the East Point Pavilion in 1993. The £1.3 million Victorian-style building stands on the site of the former Royal Hotel and contains a tourist information centre, an exhibition area and a large restaurant, in addition to the 'Discoverig', a play platform for children.

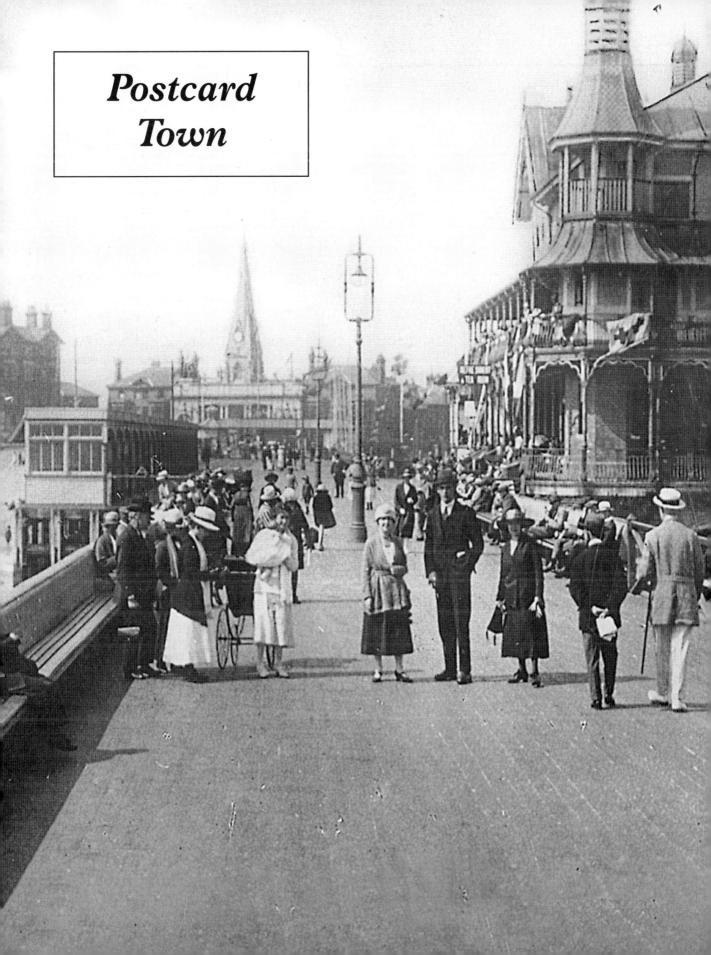

Postcard Town

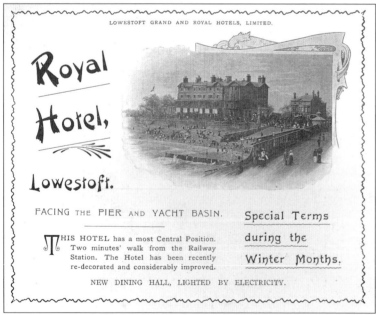

LOWESTOFT GRAND AND ROYAL HOTELS, LIMITED.

Royal
Hotel,
Lowestoft.

FACING THE PIER AND YACHT BASIN.

THIS HOTEL has a most Central Position. Two minutes' walk from the Railway Station. The Hotel has been recently re-decorated and considerably improved.

Special Terms during the Winter Months.

NEW DINING HALL, LIGHTED BY ELECTRICITY.

The Royal Hotel, with the miniature railway on the left which moved to this site in 1956. The Royal was built in 1848 by Sir Samuel Morton Peto, and as its name suggested royalty and other famous men dined at this hotel situated '... at one of the noblest Esplanades in the United Kingdom' as one 1857 guide book says. After the Second World War the Royal struggled and was demolished in 1973.

Opening in June 1900 with 200 rooms the Empire Hotel was never full and it closed at the beginning of the First World War. Subsquently the building became a hospital, known as St. Luke's, and was used by the Royal Navy during the Second World War. In 1958 the old hotel was demolished and the site bought by St. Mary's convent school.

Taking the name of an earlier coaching inn which stood further up London Road North, the Suffolk Hotel was built in 1873, and was one of the town's leading establishments of its kind during the early twentieth century. Described in 1911 as 'the most comfortable hotel in the eastern counties' as the century progressed the demand for this type of holiday accommodation waned and in November 1972 the site was redeveloped.

With an excellent sea view from Pakefield Cliff, the Grand Hotel was a 'high class establishment' which opened on Monday 10th July 1893. A popular dance hall was added in 1931, known as the 'Palais de Danse' but the hotel never re-opened after the Second World War, and in 1953 the building was taken over by compulsory purchase by the Ministry of Agriculture, Fisheries and Food. The Palais however continued until the early 1960s.

In the early 1900s the South Pier was often lined with people watching yachting, diving and swimming events. Regattas and carnivals were also held around the pier and a salt-water swimming race was contested annually from it. In 1998 the swimming race was re-established, the distance being 990 metres from the South Pier, round the Claremont Pier with a sprint finish up the beach.

View from the South Pier. Built in 1846 it wasn't until the Reading Room, on the right, was added in 1888 that the pier began to be used for pleasure rather than business purposes. The wooden structure was strengthened with concrete in 1928 and in 1956 the Reading Room was replaced by a pavilion which stood until 1989.

Overview, looking north, of the Claremont Pier and Esplanade in the late 1930s. The 670 foot pier was opened amid celebrations and a firework display in May, 1903. It was built as a stopping point for the well known Belle Fleet, which ran pleasure steamers between London and Great Yarmouth. Up until then the steamers had transferred passengers from sea to land in small boats sent out from the beach.

The Esplanade is over a mile long and seventeen yards wide with the beach on one side and a line of hotels and boarding houses on the other. Here we see it just after the Second World War, looking north towards the South Pier and pavilion, with the boating lake on the left.

Recently there has been controversy over the decision to allow cyclists access to the Esplanade but in 1957 the Official Guide to Waveney boasted that, 'Lowestoft offers all the natural facilities beloved by the younger visitor and the safe sandy beaches and broad traffic-free esplanades, with ice-cream and lollipops handy nearby, provides the fundamentals for their enjoyment ...' The guide continues, '... Lowestoft is a clean town and delights to welcome the visitor, as would the housewife to her well kept home ...'.

After the Claremont Pier was built in the early 1900s the surrounding beach became more popular and soon other attractions arrived in the vicinity such as Mr. Clarke with his goat carts. On the far right of the photograph is said to be the goat known as 'Boy Billy' which became famous for butting local dignitaries and on one occasion is even said to have attempted to chew the whiskers of the then Mayor, 'Plummy' Adams!

The South Beach, pier and pavilion. In the early days of the twentieth century mixed bathing was permitted at any time during the afternoon. You were also allowed to bathe *au naturel* protected by screens provided by the Corporation at any time before 8 a.m. and after 8 p.m.

Punch and Judy had been a part of Lowestoft beach since 1886, and here we see shows held at Children's Corner from two different eras; contending with a high tide in the 1970s (above) and in the 1930s (left). After the Second World War Mr. Franklin Spence, having retired from a lifetime in the music hall, took over the shows at Lowestoft for the next twenty years before being succeeded by Mr. Harold Woolnough, or Haraldo as he was known, who wielded Mr. Punch's stick at Children's Corner for over a decade. Since the late 1970s Professor Jingles, alias Bryan Clarke, had been continuing the tradition until he announced his retirement from the South Beach in 1999. Bryan, helped by his wife Dorothy, is a prolific maker of puppets and was a founding member of the College of Punch & Judy Professors, a select group of practitioners who try to uphold the tradition of the shows, making sure they are performed properly.

The Royal Norfolk & Suffolk Yacht Club and yacht basin on a summer's evening in the early 1990s.

The promenade on a late evening in the mid-1990s. Lowestoft seafront has seen many changes in recent years to meet the needs and changing fashions of tourism. Indeed, plans are afoot to build a multi-million pound heritage and learning centre on the South Quay, which would be the largest of its kind in East Anglia.

Harbour scene, showing a drifter passing through the opened swing bridge with, to the right, a full pleasure boat waiting to sail. At the beginning of the twentieth century many of the town's summer visitors were enchanted by the bustle of the fishing industry. 'I like Lowestoft very much,' wrote one holidaymaker in 1904, 'there are such a lovely lot of fishing drifters, smacks and trawlers. I am very fond of watching them glide out of the harbour. I have taken one sketch, but the worst of it is they will not stand still. Home on Saturday, Best of love, A.'

(Opposite) Aerial view, mid-1970s, showing the trawl dock and Waveney Drive.

Two panoramic photos of Lowestoft and its harbour in the mid-1990s. Above is the view from a crane on the extension, showing the yacht basin on the left, the trawl dock on the right and the harbour bridge in the centre. Below is another view of Lowestoft docks, this time looking seaward.

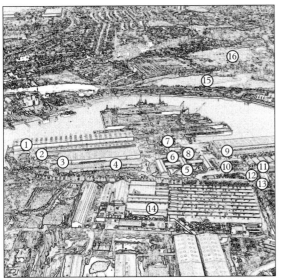

Aerial view of Brooke's South Yard in the mid-1980s.

1 'Colditz'
(Platers' shop assembly units)
2 Pipe fitters' shop
3 Platers' shop marking off
4 Laying off loft
5 Main office
6 Yard foreman's office
7 Power house
8 First Aid
9 East shop - building small
  boats in the north wing.
  Engineers, shipwrights.

10 Saw mill, joiners' shop
11 Time keeper's office
   and stores
12 Canteen
13 Drawing offices

Other Points of Interest
14 Pye T.V. factory
15 Leathe's Ham
16 Normanston Park

At noon on the 13th April 1959 the 288 ft. cargo vessel *Elk* slid into the water at her launching from the Brooke Marine shipyard. This was one of two vessels built for the Southampton - Channel Island Service for the conveyance of containers, cattle and produce.

It was under the guidance of Harry Dowsett, who took over Brooke's in 1940, that post-war international success was achieved and in the 1950s he travelled the world to win orders from Australia, Russia, the United States and Nigeria. In 1976, a year before nationalisation which saw him receive £1.8 million compensation, Dowsett spoke of the firm's proud history, stating that Brooke's had continuously built ships for seventy-six years and forty-one countries and must have been the only yard which had built vessels for both the Russian and U.S. Navies.

Privatised again in the mid-1980s, the orders dried up and Brooke Marine was wound-up but Brooke Yachts, a sister company, bought the yard and at the end of that decade enjoyed a high profile, building luxury yachts for the rich and famous. In the early 1990s cash flow problems forced job cuts and sadly closure subsequently followed.

Harry Dowsett accompanies Princess Alice at the launching ceremony of the *H.M.A.V. Ardennes* in 1976, Brooke's first ever royal launch. There was a tradition at Brooke's that the launching mistress was presented with a memento, usually a piece of jewellery. At Brooke's this was usually a cornflower, the emblem of the yard, made from gold, sapphires and diamonds but the mistresses were consulted on what would be appropriate and over the years amongst the stranger gifts given were a pair of binoculars and a fridge. Princess Alice suggested a garden seat, not such a strange request when you consider that Brooke's had a reputation for fine custom-made furniture and their craftsmen, it is said, '... did a meticulous job'.

One of the last craft to be built at Brooke's yard was the *Virgin Atlantic Challenger II*. It was officially launched 14th May 1987 with the 72 ft. motor yacht named by HRH Princess Michael of Kent before a crowd of several hundred people invited by Richard Branson, chairman of the Virgin group of companies. The £1.5 million vessel went on to win the Blue Riband for the fastest Atlantic sea crossing.

The *Ettrick* being launched at Richards' in 1991. The tradition of this yard was that the mistress, who launched the vessel, would be presented with a bouquet by a sixteen year-old apprentice.

The origins of Richards' shipbuilders date back to 1876 when Sam Richards left his home in Penzance with 25 gold sovereigns in his pocket to start a new life and business in Lowestoft. When Sam died in 1919 his three sons continued the business, confirming its reputation for innovation by building the *Veracity* in 1926, the first fully-powered motor drifter in Britain. After the Second World War Richards' continued to build trawlers and drifters and in 1957 the company was acquired by United Molasses Co. after the retirement of the two surviving brothers, Cyril and Lewis.

In the 1980s orders for minesweepers kept the yard working and in 1985 Richards' employed five hundred people but a worldwide slump in shipbuilding took its toll. The last vessel to be built at Richards' yard was the ferry *Caledonian Isles* launched by the Princess Royal in 1993, and it was failure to win the contract for another ferry which proved fatal. In April 1994 Joe Bell, managing director for almost thirty years, retired and a month later East Anglia's last remaining shipbuilder announced its closure.

The *Young Duke* LT387 heads for the fishing grounds.
This was a Richards' built diesel trawler, constructed
at the yard in 1953 for Small & Co.

The steam drifter *Loyal Friend* LT126 makes its way through the pier heads. Formerly the *Mary Flett*, this vessel was built in 1919 and owned by J. J. Colby.

Built in 1962 by Richards', the *Jacklyn* was a diesel trawler built for Jackora of Milford Haven. In 1975 this vessel was sold to the Colne Group, renamed the *Barbuda* and used for standby work before she was scrapped in 1991.

Although herring fishing in Lowestoft ceased altogether in the mid-1960s trawling has continued and today many large beam trawlers still fish out of Lowestoft. In 1999 Colne Shipping Company invested in the future of the industry with the launch of their £3 million state-of-the-art trawler the *St. Anthony*, pictured above. It's a far cry from the basic living and working conditions that fishing vessels offered earlier in the century as the *St. Anthony* is equipped with satellite systems, computer equipment, television and videos. The job has changed and the modern fisherman now has to study at college and be able to work satellite monitoring systems.

The Ranger, seen here on the left, was one of many wooden sailing trawlers (or 'smacks' as they were known locally) and is shown here being towed out to sea by the *Imperial* tug around the beginning of the century, shortly before she was stranded and wrecked on Lowestoft beach in September 1901. Smacks were gradually succeeded by steam trawlers, such as the *King Charles* (right), pictured in the 1930s, around the time that Jack's father worked on her.

Swinging the catch ashore on the fish market in the 1950s.

Salesman George Thom auctioning the day's catch to merchants at the Fish Market in the 1970s. In September 1999 a computerised fish auction was introduced here, the first if its kind in the country. Buyers will now make their bids on a keypad while foreign dealers can also join the auction via the internet. Without the shouts of the merchants the market will be a quieter place!

PICKLING HERRINGS, LOWESTOFT

The pickling plots, where the fish were gutted and packed in barrels, moved to this Hamilton Road site in the mid-1920s having previously been situated further north in Whapload Road.

(Inset, left) Fisher girls on the pickling plots, topping up the brine in the herring-filled barrels prior to export. Before this, the girls would also have gutted the herrings and packed them head to tail in the barrels, layered with salt.

A modern industrial estate has grown on the old Beach Village, where the town's fishing community lived. At the forefront of this redevelopment has been Birds Eye Walls (shown left) which opened a small depot in the town in 1949 and now has five main production units over a thirty-one acre area.

The victorious crew of the *Norfolk Yeoman*, with skipper 'Ritty' Simms on the right in the white jersey pictured in November 1963, the year they won the Prunier Trophy. This was an annual contest, first held in 1936, for drifters working from the ports of Lowestoft and Great Yarmouth with the trophy awarded to the vessel with the largest single catch of herring.

The trophy, which was presented at a celebration dinner at Madame Prunier's restaurant in London, was a marble sculpture of a hand rising out of the sea clutching a herring, and each year the name of the winning skipper, vessel and catch would be carved on its base. The winners would also receive a cash prize of £25, with the winning crew being invited to spend two days seeing the sights of London and dining at the restaurant.

Due to the decline of the herring industry, the Prunier trophy was last awarded in 1966 and has now been placed in the care of the Maritime Museum by the Herring Fishery Board.

Names & Faces

Jeannie Mary Mann, M.B.E., J.P., was born at Tunbridge Wells on 6th August 1893 and came to live in the town with her parents in 1897. A life-long member of the Methodist Church, during the First World War she worked as a school teacher at Lovewell Road. In 1918, despite opposition from her family, Miss Mann joined the Labour Party and began a long successful career in local politics, which would see her elected as Mayor in 1953. In 1962 she was awarded the M.B.E., and had a block of elderly people's flatlets in Hollingsworth Road named after her. Freeman of the Borough followed in 1970 and she remained active in public service until shortly before her death in Lowestoft Hospital on 20th February 1983.

Jack Reynolds first served as a councillor on the old Lowestoft Borough Council in 1964. A train driver by profession, he worked for British Rail for forty-seven years, and was a staunch Labour Party activist. He was elected chairman of Waveney District Council in 1993 and is pictured above wearing the chain of office. Jack Reynolds died at the age of sixty-nine in May 1995, just six days after regaining his seat in the local elections with a majority of 878.

A well known councillor and trade unionist, Ruth Ford worked at Pye T.V. Manufacturing for twenty-eight years and was awarded the gold badge - the union's highest honour - for her service to the community and the union. A member of Lowestoft Trades Council for many years, Ruth was its first female president and in 1982 she became a Waveney District Councillor, holding the seat for fifteen years during which time she was Chair of Waveney District Council. In 1998 Ruth was controversially de-selected by the local Labour Party but the following year stood as an independent candidate, narrowly losing by just fifteen votes.

Jim Prior first won the Lowestoft seat at the age of thirty-two in 1959 and held it until he retired in 1987, notching up eight election victories along the way. During his years in parliament he held a variety of important offices, including Parliamentary Private Secretary to Mr. Heath, Leader of the House of Commons, Deputy Chairman of the Conservative Party and he was Northern Ireland Secretary. When he was first elected Jim attempted to familiarise himself with his constituency's industry and had the questionable pleasure of having 'done' a twelve day trip on a deep sea trawler!

Born in Kirkley in 1948, David Porter, whose father ran a motor-cycle business in the town, was Conservative M.P. for Waveney from 1987-97. Educated at Lowestoft Grammar School and New College of Speech and Drama, David qualified as a teacher and became Head of Drama at Benjamin Britten High School in Lowestoft from 1978-81. He left teaching, trained as Conservative Party agent and was agent in Waveney before being chosen to replace Jim Prior at the 1987 General Election. In 1999 he stepped down as the Conservative Party candidate and is currently Head of Drama at Kirkley High School.

At the end of the twentieth century Bob Blizzard is Waveney's representative at Westminster. Living in Lowestoft since the early 1980s, Bob worked as a teacher in Bradwell and was also a local councillor and leader of the local Labour Party. Bob's majority in 1997 was the biggest ever win by Labour in this ward. Before this, the only time Labour had held this seat was from 1945-59 when Edward Evans won with majorities ranging from 847 to 3,332.

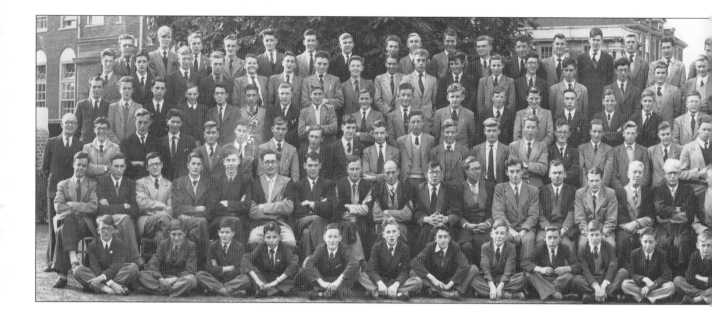

(Above and overleaf) The pupils and teachers of Lowestoft Grammar School, September 1955. Opening as Lowestoft Secondary School on 13th May 1910, the school had two hundred and fifty pupils (girls and boys were strictly segregated) and a staff of nine masters and seven mistresses. The first headmaster was J. E. B. McAllen. All but twenty-five of the pupils were fee paying and to gain a free place a scholarship had to be passed.

Mr. W. R. B. Brooks (pictured in the centre of the front row on the facing page and on page 35 at the front, second from right) served as headmaster from the mid-1930s until 1960, and oversaw many changes. In 1947 Lowestoft Secondary School became Lowestoft Grammar School, with entry by selection, the main part of which was an examination known as the 'eleven plus'. The school's first proper library opened in 1951, and long awaited extensions to the school commenced in 1956, with the building of a new craft room, assembly hall, gym block, cloakrooms, a library and cycle accommodation. Pupil numbers continued to increase in the 1960s and the school developed with tennis hard-courts laid in 1965 and the opening of a swimming-pool in 1969 which remained in use until the early 1980s. In 1970 Lowestoft Grammar School transferred to the comprehensive system and was renamed Denes High School.

Teacher Miss Howard, pictured with her class of 1929 at Pakefield School. Back row (left to right): Geoffrey Songer, Lenny Chase, Dan Baker, not known, Mary Smith, Evelyn Harper, Zillan Thacker, Henry Pegg, Alan Riches. Middle row: Florrie Peck, not known, Joan Tovell, Sadie Tripp, Brenda Sharman, Phyllis Soanes, Dora Pugh, Violet Woodrow, Megan Shales. Front row: George Crow, Owen Saunders, Alan Spendlove, Stanley Spendlove, Harry Goddard.

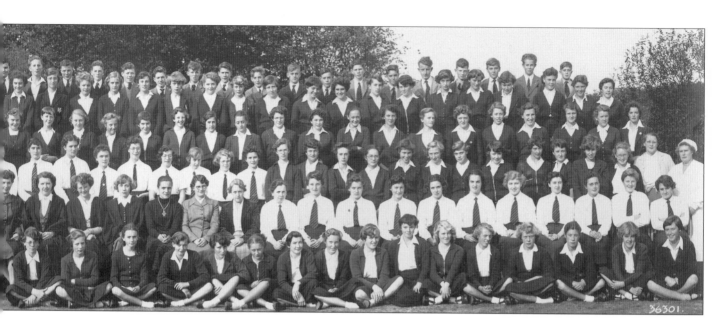

Mr. Hardman's class at Carlton Colville Primary School, 1974. Back row (left to right): Sarah Hart, Howard Aitchison, Kerry Booth. 3rd row: Teacher John Hardman, David Chipperfield, Lynn Utting, Jeanette Hook, Susan Boon, Julie Cook, Sharon Clark, Julie Clark. 2nd row: Anthea Colvin, Julie Cooke, Alison Mantripp, Tracy Catchpole, Marc Franklin, Karen Daniels, Louise Collins, Donna Parkin. Front row: Stuart Moyes, not known, David Sheldrake, Andrew Smith, Sandra Ellis, Paul Kinder, Robert Graham.

Mr. Gowan's class at Gisleham Middle School in the early 1970s. Back row: unknown, Keith Goldsmith, Gary Broom, Simon Faith, unknown, Douglas Anderton, unknown, Duncan Jones, Clive Barnard, Mr. Gowan. Middle row: student, Rosemary Ingles, Alison Meadows, Alison Clarke, Michael Lee, Stephen Cook, Nicholas Rivett, Mark Pearce, Sally Burrell, Angela Way. Front row: Joanne Middlemass, Debra Cook, Teresa Moore, Linda Hunn, Sandra Prior, Lucille Ritchie, Carol Fisk, Karen Milton, Kerry Long, Sandra Earl.

Gisleham Middle School staff photograph from the same period. The teacher's specialist area of work is referred to in brackets. Back row: Bob Pigney (Lab. Technician), student teacher, Sheila Wohlgemuth, Pam Bridges, Angela Morgan, Val Woods (Secretary), student teacher. Middle row: Graham Walsh (Music), Jim Meikle, John Hardman (Art), Brian Fookes (Geography/History), John Gowan (French), two student teachers. Front row: Diana Harold (Home Economics), John Aldridge (English), Geoff Dann (Crafts), Don Jones (Headmaster), Edna Fergusson (Deputy Head), Charles Cunningham (Maths), Mary Clarke.

The Juvenile School of Dancing in the late 1940s. Classes were held at the Adeley Hall in Junction Passage (which ran between Denmark Road and Tonning Street), where the children were taught by Miss Margaret Jones and Miss Rona Jacques. Back row (left to right): Lynn Layton, not known, Shirley Tillett, Janet Barker, Ann Whelan, Thelma Parker, Wendy Layton. Middle row: Roger Tillett, Ann Hall, Molly King, June Gooch, not known, Pat Baldry, Julian Chipperfield. Front row: Jennifer Chipperfield, Ann Baldry, Victoria Littlewood, Heather Burgess, Dawn Bunting.

Happy days at Richards' around the end of the Second World War. On the far left, with hat and glasses, can be seen Cyril Richards and on the far right, George Herring who started as an apprentice at fourteen and rose to become the managing director. In 1946 he was awarded the M.B.E. in recognition of his war work. During the last war, Richards' built 85 vessels, among them minesweepers and a number of wooden drifters for use against magnetic mines.

Crowds at a busy Lowestoft railway station on a post-war Whit Monday. At the beginning of the twentieth century, the railway station was always busy at holiday time. On a Saturday in July 1901, a large number of visitors arrived in the town and from morning till night kept the station's officials busy. Great piles of luggage were stacked upon the platform and just after midday the express arrived from London with two engines pulling twenty carriages which were packed with passengers all eager to get to the seaside. There were echoes of this in July 1999 when 3500 people arrived in the town by train for the seafront airshow with extra carriages laid on and coaches provided between Beccles and Oulton Broad.

The main assembly at Pye T.V. Manufacturing in the late 1950s. The factory, which opened in 1951, was situated in School Road on a site near to Brooke's South Yard. After Pye closed in 1981, the factory was later acquired by Sanyo industries (U.K.) Ltd.

The Modernaires was a well-known local group of entertainers who performed for audiences in the 1950s. Eddie Jessop was a comedian, Phil Wall a magician, Johnnie Orton compere, Ken Wall was the pianist, Doug Swan a ventriloquist and the Carlyle Sisters were two dancers by the name of Rona Jacques and Margaret Jones.

Singer/songwriter John Ward turned professional in 1988 and has since performed at venues all over Britain, as well as touring Germany and Southern Ireland. Born in 1964, John was educated at Kirkley High School and in the mid-1980s started performing at the Waveney Folk Club in Crown Street Hall. An accomplished musician and an energetic and passionate performer, his songs range from the thought-provoking to the humorous and John continues to write new material in a variety of styles for himself and other performers. In November 1998 John released *Waking Dreams*, his third album of his own songs.

Self-portrait of local artist Mark Burrell. Born in 1957 in Lowestoft, Mark attended a Foundation Course at Lowestoft College in 1975 but after completing his year there he decided to study on his own and as a result is a self-taught painter. His work has been seen at the Royal Academy in London and internationally in Norway and France. He has even been interviewed by Sister Wendy Beckett, one of television's most unusual art critics! Mark is one of many talented artists who live in Lowestoft, such as John Reay, Bruer Tidman and David Welch, who have all won deserved acclaim for their work and are in demand at exhibitions all over the world.

The son of a Pakefield newsagent, Michael Foreman has been a prolific and admired author and illustrator since his first picture book was published in 1961. A pupil at Notley Road (now Kirkley High School), Michael later studied at Lowestoft Art School for three years before going on to spend a year at the London School of Art. In his work he has often drawn from his memories of Lowestoft, especially in *War Boy*, published in 1989, which was about his wartime childhood in Pakefield and the sequel *After the War Was Over*, published in 1995.

The swimming pool at Nicholas Everitt's Park was home to the Oulton Broad Swimming & Diving Club who, in the late 1950s and early 1960s, won the Norfolk & Suffolk Water Polo League six times in a row. One of those victorious sides is shown here with their trophies. Top row (left to right): Terry Goldspink, Ray Wharton, John Youngman, John Garrod. Bottom row: Maurice Peters, Don Waterman, Colin 'Buster' Shears.

Lowestoft Cricket Club won the Bob Carter Cup in 1983, beating Dereham in the final. The victorious team is pictured above. Back row: David Cooper, Paul Whittaker, Mark Sellers, Bernie Haverson, Steve Tate, David Cady, Ken Duff. Front row: Kevin Cooper, Paul Rice, Doug Mattocks, Graham Martin, Brian Gale.

An annual event held in Lowestoft in the late 1990s has been the Scores Race, in which runners compete in a race held up and down the Scores. However, in the early 1900s it was walking races which were a popular event for the town's athletes. Here we see the entrants and crowds lining up for the Fish Market Walk in June 1903, shortly before the race began at 5.37 pm. Postponed on the Saturday due to bad weather the walk took place instead on Monday 29th June. The route was from Belle Vue Park corner, to Corton, then down the Long Lane, along Yarmouth Road to Gorleston railway bridge and back, a distance of fourteen miles. It is reported that the walkers '... brought out thousands to see them...' and the winner was J. Redgrave, who finished in two hours thirteen minutes, six minutes ahead of his nearest rival. He won the first prize of £5, but each of the first seven received a money award, while even eighth place won a box of cigars, with six bottles of whisky going to the fastest loser! There was even a consolation prize of free shaving and haircutting for six months to the fastest competitor over the age of thirty-five.

It seems that 'walking' had become quite a craze at the time, with the Journal reporting, 'The walk has caused desires of emulation in other quarters, and we are informed that already a contest has been arranged for the hairdressers of the borough ... It is also said that a butchers' walk is in contemplation, so altogether Lowestoft has fairly caught the fever ...'.

Paul Evans pictured in April 1996 with his medal from the London Marathon, having finished in a superb third place. This proved to be good time for Paul as the previous November he had finished second in the New York Marathon, and was also second in the Great North Run the following March. In October he went one better and won the Chicago Marathon, the biggest win of his athletics career. Paul started running seriously at the age of twenty-seven after a break of ten years and has now twice appeared at the Olympics and hopes be at the next one in Sydney in the year 2000, running the marathon for his country.

Mick Chapman, Lowestoft Town Football Club's current manager, made his debut for the club in January 1981 and went on to make 480 appearances, scoring 193 goals. At the beginning of the 1992-3 season, at the age of thirty and whilst still a formidable striker, he was appointed assistant manager, taking over as manager in a temporary capacity in January 1994 after the dismissal of Colwyn Rowe. The following season he was given the role on a permanent basis but continued as a player until a back injury forced his retirement in 1997. By then Mick's appearance record was second only to Charlie Peck who played 591 games between 1949 to 1966.

Lowestoft Town F.C. first team squad in the 1934-35 style. That season they finished second to Gorleston in the Norfolk & Suffolk League but the following year the team went one better and won the league. Back row: Chairman J. T. Cole, Frank Foster, Billy Wells, Arthur Reynolds, Harry Banks, Tommy Jones, Trainer Percy 'Putt' Gooch. Front row: Committeeman M. Shepperton, Stan Hamblin, Bert Tye, Ivan Thacker (top goalscorer with 34 goals in 34 games), Mickey Moyle, Lenny Sabberton, Fred Jones, Assistant Trainer Dick Brinson.

Lowestoft Town F.C. line up for the camera at the beginning of the 1999-2000 season. Back row: Dave Burrows, Shaun Cole (Chairman), Nigel Wilson (Physio), Jon Holmes, Micky Shade, Scott McKinney, Mark Hitcham, Jamie Stokeld, Grant Pierpoint, Colin Danby, Ian Smith, Stuart Youngman, Mick Chapman (Manager). Front row: Mike Henry, Ian Thornton, Lee Durrant, three young mascots, Sean Norman, Lee Pike, Simon Durrant.

East Suffolk Police, formed in 1840, was one of the oldest constabularies in the country and the Lowestoft Division is pictured here, lining up for the camera in 1938. Jack can remember a few of these names as the policemen who chased him when he was a boy! Back row(left to right): P.C.s C. Page, J. Botwright, C. Bedingfield, G. Robinson, A. Whitesides, F. Leeks, C. Claxton, E. Crossland, W. Shaw. Third row: P.C.s G. Smith, A. Pipe, N. Leist, E. Heard, A. Johnson, W. Sullivan, E. Frary, A. Creamer, C. Finch, A. Long, H. Blyth, K. Fancote, E. Pearce, L. Button. Second Row: P.C.s F. Gorham, E. Snell, V. Stebbings, A. Street, R. Todd, A. R. Long, W. Stammers, A. Oakes, B. Riddleston, C. Clarke, R. Chipperfield, G. Waterman, S. Goddard, G. Songer, H. Woolner. Front row: P.C.s A. Finch, A. Wightman, A. Southgate, F. Brooke, Sergeant G. Allison, Sergeant H. Rush, Sergeant L. Taylor, Inspector F. Nolloth, Superintendent H. E. Boreham, Inspector R. Hower, Inspector W. Bryant, Sergeant A. Bickers, Sergeant G. Read, Sergeant R. Furbank, P.C.s W. Bruce, B. Borley.

Reggie Stigle was Lowestoft's best known pleasure boatman for over half a century, pottering about the harbour even after his retirement in 1962. "Any more for the *Skylark*?" was his familiar shout, drumming up passengers for his small cruiser which he bought in 1936 and had originally named after his children, John and George. During the flood of January 1953 Reggie with his rowing boat rescued a group of people who were stranded in St. John's Church and the adjoining hall.

In 1969 May Elliston became Lowestoft's first female traffic warden and soon built a special relationship with the town's motorists, always approaching her job with great cheerfulness. In those days there was a platform in Station Square, a traffic control box, where traffic wardens conducted the town's cars and this led to May being dubbed the 'Toscannini' of Lowestoft traffic. For eleven years she was one of Lowestoft's favourite wardens and was described as 'not only good-humoured but sharp-eyed as well'. She had to be - on one occasion when she stopped a line of traffic, she noticed that at the head of the queue was someone sitting on her own moped. "That's my bike!" she told the surprised rider, who could only drop the bike at her feet and run away.

When May retired in October 1981 the town's traffic wardens gathered at the police station to say farewell and present her with cards and gifts. Left to right: Bill Neal, Rene Smith (holding the painting), Cecil Lord, Jack Hutson, May Elliston, Alex Knee, Leon Garrod, with Daisy Reeve holding the card, flanked by Jimmy Barker and John Ward to her right.

Above:
The Lowestoft lifeboat crew in the late 1990s. Left to right: Bert Coleman (2nd Coxswain/Mechanic) John Catchpole (Coxswain), Peter Foskett (Assistant Mechanic), Ian Brockie (crew member), C. Buckenham (Emergency Mechanic). John Catchpole has received two bronze medals in his time as Coxswain, for his service in the rescue of the crews of the *Medina D* which sank in 1988 and the *Red House Lugger* in 1997.

Left:
The Lowestoft lifeboat crew in 1930 outside their boathouse which stood on a jetty in Hamilton Dock. Coxswain Albert Spurgeon is second from the left in the front row.

Lowestoft
in the
Front Line

The town's first shock of war in the twentieth century was in October 1914, when 2,000 Belgian refugees arrived in Ostend sailing trawlers, shown here by the bridge, having fled from the Germans.

Lowestoft would be the first town in this country to be attacked by the Germans during the First World War and from 1915 Zeppelins were constantly coming and going but only on three occasions dropped bombs, one of which resulted in one casualty. The following year raids by an aeroplane and an airship thankfully came to nothing until the Easter Tuesday bombardment which took place in the early hours of April 25th, 1916, when Lowestoft was attacked from the sea by a German cruiser squadron. London Road South (left) was one of the areas of the town which received damage in the raid, which also destroyed

buildings in the Esplanade, Cleveland Road, Kirkley Run and Yarmouth Road. It was only the arrival of the Harwich flotilla which forced the German battle cruisers to stop and scatter, otherwise the town might have suffered more. As it was four people were killed and two hundred and forty properties damaged, forty of them seriously.

In September 1939 at the start of the Second World War, London schoolchildren were evacuated to Lowestoft and are pictured above at the Claremont Pier having arrived in the paddle steamer *Royal Eagle*.

Many of the London schoolchildren had already returned home by the time France was over-run by German forces in 1940 causing the east coast of Britain to be considered in danger of invasion. Plans were quickly made to get all children evacuated and now it was Lowestoft, which had received evacuees from London at the start of the war, which found itself saying goodbye to its own children as they set off by train to the villages of Derbyshire. The photograph below shows a group of Roman Hill Senior boys in Clowne, having been evacuated in June 1940. Jack Rose, pictured sitting second from the right, only stayed a month before he came home. Eventually all the children returned, some earlier than others, finding a town battle-scarred but not broken.

Sparrow's Nest became the Royal Naval Patrol Service Central Depot known as *H.M.S. Europa*. It was here that sailors came from all corners of the Empire to report for service in minesweepers, patrol ships and other naval vessels. Here we see sailors arriving with their kit bags, which provided a source of income for the local boys (below) who were paid to take the bags to the sailors' lodgings. The lads are pictured with their carts outside the main gates of Sparrow's Nest park.

The Esplanade, looking north, during the Second World War with the Royal Hotel on the left. In 1940, when a German invasion seemed imminent, the beaches and the north Denes were laid with mines and the Esplanade (above) lined with barbed wire. It wasn't until the summer of 1944, when Europe was liberated, that the restrictions on the beaches were at least partly lifted.

Photograph taken from a lecture on Lowestoft as a front line town which was given by the Air Raid Patrol Service to educate their wardens during the Second World War. It shows the corporation depot in Rotterdam Road, which was where materials such as clothing, paper and old tyres were gathered for recycling at this time of hardship and scarcity.

During the hostilities the cannons from Belle Vue Park were buried at the depot for safekeeping. After the war, they were forgotten and remained in their shallow grave until 1971 when they were found, restored and reinstalled in the park.

(Left) On the 22nd July 1941 the west side of St. Leonard's Road was destroyed in a German attack. Among the ten who died in this raid were Jack's grandmother, her sister and her sister's twin daughters.

On the 8th March 1942, Essex Road (bottom left), Eastern Way and Norfolk Street were the subject of a night raid which left one civilian dead and ten injured.

(Bottom right) A low-level morning raid by a fighter bomber killed five people on the 12th May 1943, when houses in Royal Avenue were flattened and ships were attacked outside the harbour.

(Above) During an air raid in April 1941, an undergound toilet outside the Imperial Hotel in Suffolk Road was hit and three servicemen were killed.

(Above) 5th May, 1941. Woolworth's and Timpson's were destroyed by fire during a midnight raid.

(Left) 'Sonny' Powell was on leave from the R.A.F. when he was killed with his parents in an Anderson shelter at the rear of Wollaston Road and Seago Street. The remains of the shelter can be seen scattered about in the centre of the photograph.

(Left) London Road North in 1925.

(Left, inset) The same view after 'Waller's Raid', which was the worst raid on Lowestoft in World War II. It was the 13th January 1942 and Jack remembers it well as he had just cycled past where the bombs were to fall. It was snowing and a German fighter bomber shut off his engines and came gliding out of the clouds, dropping his bombs on the town centre. There was no air-raid siren so no-one took shelter. Records show that Boot's, Waller's Restaurant, Morling's, Bonsall's, the Fifty-Shilling Tailors and Hepworth's were all hit and destroyed. Fifty-one civilians and eighteen service personnel were killed, while one person was never found. Ninety-two civilians and twenty-two service personnel were injured. In 1992, on the fiftieth anniversary of the raid, the Jack Rose Old Lowestoft Society put up a plaque in the town centre as a memorial to those who lost their lives.

(Right, top) London Road North in 1999.

(Right, bottom) The site of Bonsall's looking from London Road North towards the Marina Theatre.

In 2,075 days of war the air-raid siren was sounded at Lowestoft 2,047 times. There were ninety-three enemy raids on Lowestoft resulting in 275 people being killed and a further 684 injured.

On the 8th May 1945 the town celebrated V.E. day with street parties, such as this one in Princes Road. Lowestoft, in proportion to its size, suffered more casualties and air raid damage than any other town in the country and although the war in Europe had ended, the scars it left were in evidence in the town for many years.

London Road North, pictured on the left looking from the former site of Hepworth's shop towards the Odeon, was one of the areas left partly destroyed by bombing but gradually as rebuilding work began new shops appeared in the gaps.

(Right)
London Road North in the 1950s.

From Store to Precinct

In 1997 the Triangle Market was relocated south of its original High Street site and it is now the venue for many events and specialist markets, such as a regular Bygones Market which is held on the first Saturday of every month. This photograph was taken at the May 1999 event and featured Maypole dancing by children from a Bradwell school.

Looking up the High Street, circa 1973, with the Triangle Market on the left. The Triangle Market was first established in 1898 but only as a temporary measure because the site had been bought for the construction of a new Town Hall. When that plan was abandoned the idea to turn the area into an ornamental park caused uproar and the market stayed.

The east side of the High Street, just after the Second World War. The London Drapery (the building to the left of Edwards) is now O'Reilly's, an Irish theme pub, which secured a place in the Guiness Book of Records in 1999 for having the U.K.'s longest bar measuring at 128ft. 5inches. Edwards, the outfitters and tailors, which was one of the oldest shops in the High Street, closed in 1998, while the Albion Stores public house is now The Larder tea room. Ray Vincent, the photographer, is now next door, while Arcade Stamps and Bluebell Fashions are in the premises occupied in the photograph by the hairdressers and Ayers' the butchers.

A cat waits patiently outside the Golden Fish in St. Peter's Street. These premises had been a fishmonger's in the 1930s, before being a tool merchant's shop for a period after the Second World War. It wasn't until the 1970s, when this photograph was taken, that fresh fish was sold here again, but in more recent years this has been a music shop and a bed shop, before being converted into an office for Anglia Home Care in the late 1990s.

The Cosy Corner Picture House in the High Street (above, left) was open from 1913 to the Second World War, earning the unfortunate nickname 'the flea-pit'. Standing unoccupied for twenty years, the building was badly damaged by fire in 1960 and retail premises were eventually built on the site. Tom Watt's Ltd. was succeeded by Texas DIY store in the early 1970s remaining there until the late 1980s. In 1990 Frank Coleby Sports moved down the High Street into this building where they can still be found today.

Sizzers hairdressers, pictured above in 1999, and on the left in July 1982, are situated next door to Coleby's at 106 High Street. Established by Dennis Lines in Regent Road in 1966, the business moved in 1979 to these premises, which are shown (above left) when occupied by Home Radio after the Second World War. In the early 1960s a dress shop moved in but Proteus Carpets could be found at the address the following decade. In the 1930s Francis' Fruit Shop traded here, owned by Mr. Meridan Smith for whom Jack used to run errands.

W. E. Turner's and Rogers' Bookshop, just after the Second World War. Turner's shoe shop remained here until the late 1960s before moving down into London Road North. Rogers' bookshop started off in London Road North but after the war was run by Mr. D. S. Mitchley and his son, Jack, at 91 High Street until the early 1950s. Bettatravel and Lowestoft Beds are are now located in these buildings.

In the early 1900s this glass, china and earthenware warehouse was situated at No. 85 High Street and was a typical shop of its day. This building suffered bomb damage during World War II and was demolished in 1956. In recent years The Mart and Allen's Music have occupied the rebuilt premises.

Tonning Street, pictured just before the First World War, was a busy shopping centre at this time. There were three grocers, three butchers plus two pork butchers, two greengrocers, two hairdressers, two confectioners, two saddlers, two 'shopkeepers', two fishmongers, a printer, a pharmacist, a furnishing store, a tobacconist, a beer retailer, a bird-fancier's shop, a carpenter, a house decorator, a dressmaker and a life assurance company. Also, one Ernest William Gunn had premises in which he was an electrical engineer, heating and power contractor, musical instrument dealer and corn chandler.

In 1951 Ernest Prentice and his wife Irene, took over a greengrocery business at 122 St. Peter's Street in premises now occupied by a chemist. Gradually they began to sell more grocery items as shops around them closed and their mobile van (shown on the left) served the Gunton Estate in the days before the Hollingsworth Road shopping parade was built. In 1971 the Prentice family moved to Kessingland and opened a supermarket by which time both their sons, Ivan and Austin, had joined the family business which expanded into neighbouring shops. After Ernest's death in 1985, a decision was made to knock the three separate shops into one. In 1995 this was sold and the following year another shop was opened in Carlton Colville where they still pride themselves on personal service. "The shops of independent grocers had character, personality, quick and friendly service, a large variety of produce and a sympathetic ear for customers' troubles," said Ernest Prentice in 1966 when he was president of the local Grocers' Association. "Good service did not begin with 2d. off"

In the early 1900s Alfred George Cutts, baker and confectioner, had these premises in Beaconsfield Road and another shop in nearby St. Leonard's Road. In the 1920s the business moved to 177 London Road South and remained there until the Second World War.

The Beaconsfield Road premises have been put to a variety of uses since the 1920s and more recently have been both a hairdressing salon and a butchers.

Britain's most easterly Post Office is situated in Lowestoft's High Street and has been run by Michael and Elaine Leslie since May 1996. Redesigned in 1998, this Post Office was built in the early 1930s on the former site of a hatter's which was destroyed during the German bombardment in the First World War.

Nos. 207-211 London Road South just after the Second World War, showing (left to right) Boot's Chemists, Freeman Hardy & Willis and Stafford's the tobacconists. Freeman Hardy & Willis also had another branch in London Road North. Currently these three premises are occupied by Olympic Print, a Chinese takeaway and Streetlife Cycles.

Hailey's in London Road South was one of the town's finest department stores. In the early hours of Saturday March 22nd, 1980, these premises were damaged by a fire which was tackled by forty firemen with eight appliances. Although the blaze was confined to one area of the store, it resulted in all the stock being covered in smoke and an oily grime. Initially it was hoped that the shop would re-open within three weeks but it never did and the building stood empty for many years. Hailey's Court, a block of flats, now stands on the site.

Pier Terrace, situated on the west side of the approach to the bridge, seen less encumbered with traffic in the 1950s. Ford Jenkins had a shop in this row at the time, next door to the Lowestoft Bedding Centre on the left, while the confectioners on the right, Butter Creams Ltd., had been situated here since the mid-1920s.

Bevan Street in 1980. This is one of the town's busy secondary shopping areas and always has a diverse range of shops. Oxfam still occupy the same shop today and there is still an optician next door. Capaldi's, established as a cafe after the war, later became a gift shop under the same name and currently these premises are the Red Cross charity shop. The next two buildings now house Crocodile Rock and a mobile phone shop.

The west side of London Road North circa 1880. Gordon Road, which was cut in 1883, now runs across this area. It was in the 1880s that many of the fine residences in London Road North, where prosperous boat owners and eminent local businessmen had lived, began to give way to shops and commerce.

A horse and cart makes its way down a snowy London Road North around the beginning of the twentieth century, with the beginning of the High Street seen in the distance. Tesco's store is now situated on the left. The premises of Ashford's Travel Bureau (see facing page) would be situated near the street light.

The east side of London Road North, 1999. The buildings on the right, up to Gordon Road, were all erected in the second half of the twentieth century, but both the Central Methodist Church, demolished in 1956, and Catlings, which came down in 1980, had once stood in this row. The distinctive town clock was put up in 1983, while the pedestrian precinct was opened on 1st August 1985 by H.M. the Queen who unveiled a plaque officially naming the area Queen Elizabeth II Place.

A florist's, a sports shop, a greengrocer's and currently, a clothes shop, have all since been at these premises at 126 London Road North. In the 1920s Frederick Charles Ashford, pictured in the doorway, ran his emigration and shipping office here. Around the same period, Mr. Ashford was also proprietor of a restaurant at 87-89 London Road North (now the site of W. H. Smith's) and a temperance hotel in Waveney Road.

The east side of London Road North, now and then, in the 1970s (left) and at the end of the twentieth century (above).

London Road North west side, now and then. By the early 1980s (right) traffic was removed from the town centre but the old road had yet to be dug up and paved. In 1999 (above) the only cars are on the fairground rides for children which are situated here.

Tuttle's, pictured above in the 1950s, closed in 1981, but had ceased to be a family run business in 1960 when it was bought by Debenhams and later Brahams in 1972. Four generations of the Tuttle family were concerned in the running of the firm over a 117 year period, from its beginnings at 66 High Street in 1843, moving several times until in November 1886 the company purchased a plot of land from the proprietors of the Grove Estate and erected the commanding business premises bearing the name Bon Marché. In 1888 the Lowestoft Journal heralded the arrival of '... one of the largest shops in the town (if not the largest)...'. It went on to describe the ground floor as '... one of the most excellently arranged and commodious business areas to be found in the entire neighbourhood and cannot fail to strike the beholder especially as he approaches the place especially by the grand entrance at the junction of the London with the Suffolk Road ...'.

The Journal continued, '... Looking then at both the exterior and interior of the Bon Marché it would seem that spirited proprietors have been deterred by no expense in order to make the establishment worthy of their own reputation, as well as an ornament to the locality in which it is placed; and while the outlay involved must have been very considerable, yet they anticipate a corresponding return commensurate therewith, and if civility, attention, and readiness to oblige will insure it, we have little doubt of their success ...'.

Chadd's are the town's biggest independent store. Established in 1907 by G. B. Chadd, part of the building was originally Flood's the stationers (shown right) which was later the Coronet cinema. Chadd's always do well in the 'Lowestoft In Bloom' competition and in 1999 was awarded a silver medal for the colourful array of flowers decorating their shop front (which can be seen above) being narrowly beaten in the commercial section of the event by Salveson's Food Services.

A mid-1970s bird's eye view of Lowestoft showing the Stella Maris Church and St. John's Church on the right with the old bus station and the rear of the Odeon cinema below.

A Bird's Eye View

Looking over the rooftops from Lowestoft College in 1999, towards the Co-op factory chimney, which is due for demolition, and the grain silo on the left. Below is the opposite view, taken from the silo, showing the 'harbour village'. Clemence Street and Selby Street are the two main vertical roads, while Denmark Road runs across the photograph in the foreground. Lowestoft College is the big building which can be seen in the distance on the right, behind Roman Hill School, while St. Margaret's Church and its spire can be found in the centre of the horizon.

Another view from the College, showing the Crown Meadow football ground, the Drill Hall on the left, and in the centre of the photograph is the tower of the Stella Maris Church with the sea in distance.

The town's only tower block, St. Peter's Court, dominates this view of North Lowestoft, with an unusually quiet St. Peter's Street running through the centre of this photograph. The Italian style tower of the Town Hall and clock can be seen left of centre in the skyline.

View from the Stella Maris Church in the mid-1980s (above) and the late 1950s (below), with Clapham Road running centrally across the photograph. In July 1940 a direct hit during an air raid destroyed the Co-operative Stores shop which stood on the corner of Clapham Road and Gordon Road. This was one of many bomb sites in the town which stood undeveloped for many years. Demolition of another kind occurred in the mid-1970s when the east side of Clapham Road was demolished to make way for the new one-way system.

View from the top of St. Peter's Court in 1977. The St. Peter's Street roundabout was being built at this time as part of the one-way system. Where this roundabout and roads were laid a whole community had lived. The picture on the right shows the backyard of a house in Mariner's Street, one of the many roads in this area which was demolished in the 1950s as part of the slum clearance programme.

Lowestoft docks, July 1999, with Hamilton Dock on the left and Waveney Dock on the right with part of the new Fish Market in the foreground. In the centre of the photograph can be seen the old 'T-piece' which was where the drifters used to land. Since April 1999 this has been the place where rock has been unloaded from Sweden and France by cargo ships. The rocks are then taken by a barge, which is shown loading up on the photograph, to the Norfolk coast, near Caister, where work is being carried out to build up the sea defences.

The picture below is the same view in the 1970s. On the left can be seen the fish sheds which were demolished as part of an improvement scheme in the mid-1980s.

View overlooking Waveney Dock and the old Fish Market in the 1970s, showing the premises of the Ice Company on the right. The conveyor belt which extends from their building to the dock carries ice to awaiting vessels for packing fish at sea. This is still in use although the Fish Market was refurbished in the mid-1980s, with improvements made to existing facilities and the construction of a new auction hall and fish processing area. Although the Fish Market is not normally open to the public, a bi-annual Fish Fayre is held there which attracts large crowds.

(Above) A trawler passes through the opened swing bridge in this mid-1920s view of the harbour area. However, the traffic seems surprisingly sparse compared with today; on the south side there seems to be only a tram waiting for the bridge to close again.

(Left)
There are about thirty-five years between the upper photograph, taken in the mid-1990s, and the one below, circa 1960. Among the things missing in the later shot are the Royal Hotel, Palace Cinema, the Suffolk Hotel, South Pier Pavilion, St. John's Church, the swing bridge and harbour cottages. The grain silo, which seems to dominate most aerial photographs of the town, can't be found in the earlier scene as it wasn't built until 1962 and on the Old Extension the shingle mill has already gone, demolished in 1958, but the railway lines leading to it are still in place. The extension is currently used for the construction of oil rig modules, which can be seen in the foreground of the later view.

The South Beach, Claremont Pier, the Esplanade, Marine Parade and London Road South, in 1979.

The spire of St. John's Church had always been a landmark. Mariners used it to fix their position at sea, and during World War Two attempts were made to camouflage it to foil German bombers.

South Lowestoft 1979. With the vacant sites of the Royal Hotel (on the left) and St. John's Church, demolished two years earlier (centre right), it was something of a transitional period for this area. A traffic warden can be seen bravely directing the traffic at the bottom of London Road South, which is now controlled by traffic lights. A road, joining Marine Parade (left) and Belvedere Road, has also been built.

Aerial view of Oulton Broad in the mid-1980s. In the foreground can be seen the *Yellow Tail*, which for many years lay submerged near Mutford Bridge as attempts were made to contact its owner. The railway bridge is on the right and the two railway lines which dissect Oulton Broad can be seen with the North Station visible near the roundabout at the top of the photograph. Shortly after this picture was taken, in 1986, it was announced that the bridge was to be closed to heavy goods vehicles because it had been carrying much more traffic than it had been designed for and in February 1991 work began on the new bascule bridge and road to take traffic away from the congested centre of Oulton Broad.

Oulton Broad in 1979. Nicholas Everitt's Park is in the centre of the photograph, surrounded by the trees, with the swimming pool on the right. Bridge Road can be followed right up to the junction of Cotmer Road and Beccles Road and the unusual roof of the *Flying Dutchman* public house can be made out in the distance towards the left. Carlton and its marshes lie further afield. The route of the new relief road, Saltwater Way, runs through the left of the photograph, where the trees can be seen.

Oulton Broad in the late 1970s, with the club house of the Oulton Broad Motorboat Club on the left of the photograph. Formed in 1933 by a small band of local businessmen, the club has grown and made motorboat racing synonymous with Oulton Broad.

(Left)
A mid-50s photo-graph with driver Mick Pickering facing the camera.

A Sense
of Place

The origins of the Marina Theatre date back to 1878 when a roller skating rink was built on this site, with a makeshift stage erected for the performance of plays or dances. In 1896 the rink was converted into a theatre with the first show 'Jim the Penman' performed by the Haymarket Drama Society opening on the 26th April the following year. With the advent of talkies the Marina Theatre became a cinema in the 1930s and at the end of the twentieth century it continues to provide the town with a variety of entertainment from films and plays to comedy acts and musical shows.

At the beginning of the twentieth century providing the townspeople with a central recreation ground was seen as a priority for the future. The Denes Oval, pictured above, was laid out in 1925 on land that had been allotments, and included a cricket pitch and tennis courts. With a nearby golf club opening the following year and an open air swimming pool which had been built in the early 1920s, the Denes was the place to be for sporting activities. The swimming pool was damaged during the Second World War and later filled in to become part of the caravan site which had been first established on the Denes in the late 1920s.

For many years it had been Jack Rose's dream to open a war museum in the town, dedicated to all those who served in or from the Lowestoft area during the Second World War. In the early 1990s the dream suddenly became a possibility when he was offered a building in Sparrow's Nest Park by Waveney District Council. The only problem was the building's dilapidated condition and it took a lot of work by Jack and an enthusiastic team of volunteers and friends before the museum finally opened on 7th May, 1995. Jack, pictured here outside the museum's main entrance, will always be grateful to those who helped him achieve his dream and also to those who continue to support the museum today.

95

The lighthouse pictured in 1980, five years after it became fully automatic. Lowestoft lays claim to having the first lighthouse in the country in 1609, although before this warning lights were provided by bonfires, braziers and beacons to help mariners. The beacon from the tower can now be seen for a 23 mile radius at sea, flashing every fifteen seconds. In 1997 the lighthouse was modernised but recently there were fears that the light was to be extinguished when a 'for sale' notice appeared in front of the old building. However, only the keeper's cottage is for sale and the future of the tower is assured - it seems that the Lowestoft lighthouse will go on shining well into the new century.

The *Spirit of Lowestoft* (left) has been stationed in the town since November 1987 when it was bought with money raised by the people of Lowestoft. The photograph below shows the view from Lowestoft's lifeboat during the rescue of the *Red House Lugger*, the tiny yacht which can be seen between the Aldeburgh lifeboat and the large vessel on the right. The yacht, with two adults and four children aboard, was damaged in these atrocious weather conditions thirty miles S.E. of Lowestoft on the 29th August, 1996. The Aldeburgh boat moved in first and managed to take off three of the passengers. Lowestoft's Second Coxswain Bert Coleman then went aboard to take charge of the yacht and in a force eleven wind with a seven metre swell, the *Spirit of Lowestoft,* under Coxswain John Catchpole's command, drew alongside the yacht close enough for the crew to be pulled aboard to safety. For his service in this rescue, John Catchpole received the R.N.L.I.'s bronze medal.

The Duchess of Kent opened the new fire station in Normanston Drive on 3rd June 1972. Known as the Normanhurst Station, the name derives from the Victorian mansion which was requisitioned by the National Fire Service during the Second World War and became home to the local fire service for thirty years. The new station was built in front of the old house, which was then demolished when the building work was completed. Considered to be one of the finest stations in the country at the time of its erection, its future is now in the balance due to high running costs with the building of a new fire station being considered.

When Normanhurst Mansion was the town's fire station the firemen had to rush out of the building and cross a roadway to reach the appliances. The photograph (below) shows firemen Barry Scaplehorn, George Challis, Peter Keating, Jack Hutson and 'Lofty' Rackham racing to a call in 1970. The photograph (above) shows the old Normanhurst appliance bay with a water tender about to leave. On the left can be seen the rescue tender which the station had painted yellow before the Home Office insisted it was changed back to its original colour of red.

Lowestoft, summer 1999, with Christ Church on the right flanked by the industrial estate which has grown around it since the Second World War. On the left can be seen the Magistrates' Court, with the Police Station behind it. The station, which opened in June 1979, is a four-storey building which cost £1¼ millon to construct, standing over more than an acre.

For over a century the home of Lowestoft's constabulary was in Regent Road. Patched up after the war, by the early 1970s the building had become too small for its use. Due to the increase in size of the local division, it was re-organised in October 1972 and at this time had 220 officers, 58 motor vehicles in use including 6 patrol cars, 4 motor cycles, 6 panda cars, 18 beat vans, and 8 traffic wardens. By the late 1970s, at the time this picture was taken, plans were afoot for a new station.

Lowestoft's Police Station (the building to the left of the photograph) was left badly damaged during wartime bombing but continued to be used as a report centre although the main operation moved into Church Road School. The old mansion house to the rear of the station in Regent Road, which had been the previous headquarters in the mid-nineteeth century, was completely destroyed by the bomb.

The Council chamber was part of the original Town Hall which was built in 1857 and contains three fine stained-glass windows, one of which is shown in the photograph. These windows were the gift of Sir Samuel Morton Peto, who was a major figure in the history of the town and its development. The largest of these windows commemorates the alliance of England and France against Russia in the Crimean War and before they were put in place in the town chamber they were exhibited in France where many thousands of people gathered to see them.

The Town Hall in the High Street, around the time of the First World War. The Town Hall was erected in 1857 but in 1899 was set back ten feet for the widening of the High Street. 'The addition of the oak panelling and the provision of a platform and a new entrance are admirable,' noted one commentator in 1900, 'I have no doubt the present building will serve the town for at least twenty five years ...'.

St. Margaret's Church was built in the late fifteenth century on the site of an older church of which only the fifty foot tower remains, topped with a seventy foot spire. Surviving the centuries, the Parish Church even escaped bombing during World War II. However, in March 1941, due to the threat of invasion, the church plate was hidden and buried under a tomb. Five years later, on 31st March 1945, the plate was dug up and used at the Communion Service the following day, Easter Sunday.

Although the twentieth century has seen the demolition of churches in the town, such as St. John's, the Central Methodist and St. Peter's Church, new places of worship have been built, among them London Road Baptist, the Free Presbyterian and Trinity Methodist (right). Situated opposite the lighthouse, Trinity Methodist was opened in September 1970, built with the proceeds from the sale of Tonning Street Methodist Church and the High Street Methodist Church.

Lowestoft Railway Station in the 1970s. In the days when the bridge was under the control of British Railways a warning bell was rung at the station when the bridge went up so that the train could be delayed, and even in the late 1950s the bridge wasn't opened in the ten minutes before a train left the station. When it became necessary to remove the glass roof which had become structurally unsound, fears grew for the station's future, but the interior was redesigned and in 1999 it was nominated as a finalist in Railtrack's station of the year competition.

In 1973 Lowestoft Fish Market severed its links with the railway when the transportation of offal was switched to the road and the tracks which ran from the market to the station were removed. This ended a tradition which dated back to the 1st May 1855 when 43 drifters landed 130 lasts of herrings which filled 54 railway trucks for despatch to London and the Midlands.

In the early 1970s a temporary retractable bridge (pictured above) carried the town's traffic and pedestrians over the harbour until a new structure could be built to replace the old swing bridge, which had jammed in the open position in January 1969. During the 1960s the swing bridge had become unreliable and was stuck regularly, and as early as 1961 the town's trade unionists threatened to strike if something wasn't done about the problem. One of the ideas put forward at the time was to construct a fly-over bridge running from Waveney Drive to Normanston Drive but the estimated cost of £1 million was considered too expensive.

Although Oulton Broad (above) is a popular holiday centre and busy with leisure boats and watersports, it can also be the setting for a tranquil sunset such as this.

The Broad House Museum (left) is situated in Nicholas Everitt's Park and was opened on the 1st August 1985 by H.M. Queen Elizabeth II and H.R.H. The Duke of Edinburgh. Previously located in the Prairie, now the site of the Britten Centre, the museum is full of exhibits relating to the town's history, including a large display of Lowestoft porcelain and a case containing the mayoral robes and regalia. Broad House itself has a rich history and the first record of the building dates back to 1685. In the early twentieth century it was home to Nicholas Everitt, a solicitor, writer and sportsman, after whom the park would be named following his death in 1928.

Named after the composer Benjamin Britten who was born in the town, the Britten Centre features a market which is open several days a week.

A well attended French market was held on the Triangle over a bank holiday weekend in May 1999.

Clapham Road, circa 1916, with the Carnegie Library on the right. Opening in May 1905, this library received a direct hit in an air raid in March 1941. Three-quarters of the books were salvaged and subsequently the library was moved to St. Andrew's Hall and then to Eastholme in the High Street before moving to premises in Suffolk Road in 1951.

Looking north over the old swing bridge in the late 1950s. Mr Ron Ashby, who kindly lent us some of his postcards for this book, was surprised to recognise the Caley's and Morgan's lorry that he drove on the left of the photograph. When this bridge was opened in June 1897 it was considered to be a wonderful piece of engineering and design but the structure soon attracted criticism that it was too narrow with people complaining that there wasn't enough room for two carts to pass. Apparently lorries would later have a similar problem!

Lowestoft's current library was built on the site of the old Carnegie Library and opened on Saturday 22nd February, 1975. Since then it has kept abreast of technology and the complete catalogue of books available throughout Suffolk libraries is fully computerised and internet access and word processing facilities are available.

Lowestoft's present bridge struggles to cope with the demands of modern traffic but in 1988, after a long campaign for a new harbour crossing, it was announced that a second bridge would be in place by the summer of 1994 only for the project to be duly shelved. "There is no doubt that Lowestoft has a great need for a third crossing," deputy County Surveyor David Gardner had said in 1985, but warned, "it will not be less than five years and you will be lucky if you can get it inside fifteen years ..."

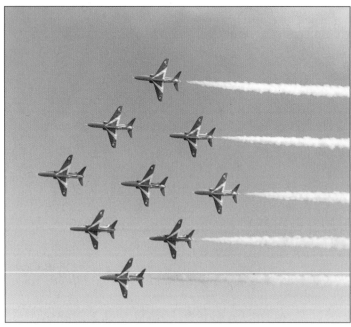

The crowds start to gather on Lowestoft's South Beach in July 1999 for the beginning of Lowestoft's third annual seafront air show. Holidaymakers and locals flocked to see some of the world's most impressive flying displays and an estimated 140,000 people visited the town during the festival. The photograph on the left shows the Red Arrows display team in action at the town's most succesful air show yet.

Wellington Esplanade and the restored Wellington Gardens, which were opened in July 1999. The original sunken garden was destroyed during the Second World and an air raid shelter put in its place, and trenches were dug throughout the rest of the gardens. Filled in and patched up after the war, in 1997 it was decided to try to restore the gardens in keeping with their Victorian tradition. It was in 1856 when Wellington Esplanade was built by Sir Samuel Morton Peto, and the gardens, which were originally called Wellington Lawn, still run the entire length of the terrace and will once again be a blaze of colour.

A feature of the newly laid Wellington Gardens are two large bronze plaques, depicting Sir Morton Peto's contribution to the town. Cast from moulds made by Ernie Childs of Great Yarmouth Potteries, these were paid for in part by the Jack Rose Old Lowestoft Society.

Unique to Lowestoft, the 'Scores' are alleyways which lead down from the High Street to Whapload Road where the Beach Village was once situated. At one time there were twelve Scores but in the late 1970s Frost's Alley Score was built over during the construction of the new Police Station, and Maltsters Score (pictured right) and Wilde's Score have been halved. Now diverted into Spurgeon Score, Maltsters had a poor reputation in Victorian times and robberies were frequent here.

The picture shows the cottages and crinkle-crankle walls which could once be found in the Score. By the 1990s there was only a small section of these wavy walls still standing - the cottages have long been demolished - but in 1999 Maltsters Score was one of the Scores which was refurbished and more crinkle-crankle walls were built.

Wilde's Score takes its name from John Wilde, who died in 1738 leaving all his money to start a school which was situated within this Score. Most of the school buildings were destroyed in an air raid during World War II and subsequently the school never re-opened but one remaining school room, a Victorian structure, which in the 1980s had been used by Birds Eye for personnel training, was given to the Lowestoft Civic Society in 1995 for use as a Heritage Centre. The Society have been working hard to refurbish the premises and have recently been awarded a lottery grant to enable them to continue the renovation.

Station Square was one of the many areas of town which suffered from flooding when a month's rainfall fell in less than two hours on Monday 9th August 1999. The conditions, which forced dozens of town centre shops, cafes and offices to close and left many roads unpassable, evoked memories of the 1953 flood. Torrential rain also hit Lowestoft the day before and threatened to wash out the town's annual carnival.

St. John's Road, which was one of the areas which suffered in the downpour of August 1999, is pictured here the day after the floods of January 1953. This was caused by a combination of high tides and a strong wind, which resulted in the sea inundating properties all over town, devastating homes and shops, giving the locals a night they wouldn't forget.

The sun sets over the
most easterly town.

Picture Index